The Complete

LIFE'S LITTLE
INSTRUCTION BOOK™

H. Jackson Brown, Jr.

Rutledge Hill Press
Nashville, Tennessee

Published in Nashville, Tennessee, by Rutledge Hill Press, Inc., 211 Seventh Avenue North, Nashville, Tennessee 37219. Distributed in Canada by H.B. Fenn and Co., Ltd., 34 Nixon Road, Bolton, Ontario L7E 1W2. Distributed in Australia by Millennium Books, 33 Maddox Street, Alexandria NSW 2015. Distributed in New Zealand by Tandem Press, 2 Rugby Road, Birkenhead, Auckland 10.

Design by Gary Gore
Typography by D&T/Bailey Typesetting, Inc., Nashville, Tennessee

Library of Congress Cataloging-in-Publication Data

Brown, H. Jackson, 1940–
    [Life's little instruction book]
    The complete life's little instruction book / H. Jackson Brown, Jr.
      p.   cm.
    Originally published in 3 vols. : Life's little instruction book.
    Nashville, Tenn. : Rutledge Hill Press, c1991–c1995.
        ISBN 1-55853-490-3
    1. Happiness—Quotations, maxims, etc.   2. Conduct of life—
Quotations, maxims, etc.   I. Title.
[BJ1481.B87   1997]
170'.44—dc21

97-5575
CIP

Printed in the United States of America
3 4 5 6 7 8 9 — 01 00 99 98

INTRODUCTION

A lot has happened since the fall of 1990 when I sat at our kitchen table and jotted down a few pages of instructions and personal observations for my son, Adam. He was beginning his freshman year at college, and I felt that a collection of the insights and discoveries which had positively influenced my own life might be an appropriate gift to commemorate this important event.

As a young adult, Adam would soon find himself standing at life's most challenging crossroads. His choosing the right path would make all the difference. Here was my attempt to help his heart as well as his head to know the way.

Introduction

That first list of fatherly advice contained 511 entries. I mailed him a new collection every two years. These lists were published as little books, and to my surprise and delight became bestsellers.

But Adam and I are most proud of the fact that this correspondence between us is now available in 28 languages and is valued by others throughout the world as a cherished reference and useful guide.

This new edition brings together all three volumes of *Life's Little Instruction Book* and offers them in what I think is a most handsome package. The rich, dark leather binding and gold embossing certainly make the contents appear important. But Adam tells me he has always thought so. After reading a few pages, I hope you'll agree.

H. J. B.
Tall Pine Lodge
Fernvale, Tennessee

Son, how can I help you see?
May I give you my shoulders to stand on?
Now you see farther than me.
Now you see for both of us.
Won't you tell me what you see?

Other Books by H. Jackson Brown, Jr.

A Father's Book of Wisdom
P.S. I Love You
Life's Little Instruction Book
Live and Learn and Pass It On
Life's Little Instruction Book, Volume II
Life's Little Instruction Book, Volume III
Life's Little Treasure Book on Joy
Life's Little Treasure Book on Marriage and Family
Life's Little Treasure Book on Wisdom
Life's Little Treasure Book on Success
Life's Little Treasure Book on Parenting
Life's Little Treasure Book on Love
Life's Little Treasure Book on Hope
Life's Little Treasure Book on Friendship
Life's Little Treasure Book of Christmas Traditions
When You Lick a Slug, Your Tongue Goes Numb
The Little Book of Christmas Joys
(with Rosemary Brown and Kathy Peel)
Live and Learn and Pass It On, Volume II
Live and Learn and Pass It On, Volume III
A Hero in Every Heart (with Robyn Spizman)

VOLUME ONE

1 Compliment three people every day.

2 Have a dog.

3 Watch a sunrise at least once a year.

4 Remember other people's birthdays.

5 Overtip breakfast waitresses.

6 Have a firm handshake.

7 Look people in the eye.

8 Say "thank you" a lot.

9 Say "please" a lot.

10 Learn to play a musical instrument.

11 Sing in the shower.

12 Use the good silver.

13 Learn to make great chili.

14 Plant flowers every spring.

15 Own a great stereo system.

16 Be the first to say, "Hello."

17 Live beneath your means.

18 Buy great books, even if you never read them.

19 Drive inexpensive cars, but own the best house you can afford.

20 Be forgiving of yourself and others.

21 Learn three clean jokes.

22 Wear polished shoes.

23 Floss your teeth.

24 Drink champagne for no reason at all.

25 Ask for a raise when you feel you've earned it.

26 Buy whatever kids are selling on card tables in their front yard.

27 If in a fight, hit first and hit hard.

28 Return all the things you borrow.

29 Teach some kind of class.

30 Be a student in some kind of class.

31 Never buy a house without a fireplace.

32 Once in your life own a convertible.

33 Treat everyone you meet like you want to be treated.

34 Learn to identify the music of Chopin, Mozart, and Beethoven.

35 Plant a tree on your birthday.

36 Donate two pints of blood every year.

37 Make new friends but cherish the old ones.

38 Keep secrets.

39 Take lots of snapshots.

40 Never refuse homemade brownies.

41 Don't postpone joy.

42 Ask someone to pick up your mail and daily paper when you're out of town. Those are the first two things potential burglars look for.

43 Never give up on
anybody. Miracles
happen every day.

44 Write "thank you" notes promptly.

45 Show respect for teachers.

46 Show respect for police officers and firefighters.

47 Show respect for military personnel.

48 Don't waste time learning the "tricks of the trade." Instead, learn the trade.

49 Keep a tight rein on your temper.

50 Buy vegetables from truck farmers who advertise with hand-lettered signs.

51 Put the cap back on the toothpaste.

52   Take out the garbage without being told.

53   Avoid overexposure to the sun.

54   Vote.

55   Surprise loved ones with little unexpected gifts.

56   Stop blaming others. Take responsibility for every area of your life.

57   Never mention being on a diet.

58   Make the best of bad situations.

59   Learn to make something beautiful with your hands.

60 Live so that when your children think of fairness, caring, and integrity, they think of you.

61 Support a high school band.

62 Admit your mistakes.

63 Use your wit to amuse, not abuse.

64 Remember that all news is biased.

65 Take a photography course.

66 Let people pull in front of you when you're stopped in traffic.

67 Always accept an outstretched hand.

68 Be brave. Even if you're
not, pretend to be.
No one can tell
the difference.

69 Demand excellence and be willing to pay for it.

70 Whistle.

71 Hug children after you discipline them.

72 Give to charity all the clothes you haven't worn during the past three years.

73 Never forget your anniversary.

74 Eat prunes.

75 Ride a bike.

76 Choose a charity in your community and support it generously with your time and money.

77 Slow dance.

78 Steer clear of restaurants with strolling musicians.

79 Don't take good health for granted.

80 When someone wants to hire you, even if it's for a job you have little interest in, talk to them. Never close the door on an opportunity until you've had a chance to hear the offer in person.

81 Don't mess with drugs, and don't associate with those who do.

82 Avoid sarcastic remarks.

83 In business and in family relationships, remember that the most important thing is trust.

84 Forget the Joneses.

85 Never encourage anyone to become a lawyer.

86 Don't smoke.

87 Even if you're financially well-to-do, have your children earn and pay part of their college tuition.

88 Even if you're financially well-to-do, have your children earn and pay for *all* their automobile insurance.

89   Recycle old newspapers, bottles, and cans.

90   Refill ice cube trays.

91   Never invest more in the stock market than you can afford to lose.

92   Choose your life's mate carefully. From this one decision will come ninety percent of all your happiness or misery.

93   Make it a habit to do nice things for people who'll never find it out.

94   Lend only those books you never care to see again.

95 Don't let anyone ever see you tipsy.

96 Attend class reunions.

97 Always have something beautiful in sight, even if it's just a daisy in a jelly glass.

98 Know how to type.

99 Read the Bill of Rights.

100 Learn how to read a financial report.

101 Tell your kids often how terrific they are and that you trust them.

102 Take a brisk thirty-minute walk every day.

103 Think big thoughts, but relish small pleasures.

104   Use credit cards only for convenience, never for credit.

105   Treat yourself to a massage on your birthday.

106   Never cheat.

107   Smile a lot. It costs nothing and is beyond price.

108   Know how to drive a stick shift.

109   Spread crunchy peanut butter on Pepperidge Farm Gingerman cookies for the perfect late-night snack.

110   Never use profanity.

111 When dining with clients or business associates, never order more than one cocktail or one glass of wine. If no one else is drinking, don't drink at all.

112 Never argue with police officers, and address them as "officer."

113 Learn to identify local wildflowers, birds, and trees.

114 Keep a fire extinguisher in your kitchen and car.

115 Give yourself a year and read the Bible cover to cover.

116 Consider writing a living will.

117 Install dead bolt locks on outside doors.

118 Don't buy expensive wine, luggage, or watches.

119 Put a lot of little marshmallows in your hot chocolate.

120 Learn CPR.

121 Resist the temptation to buy a boat.

122 Stop and read historical roadside markers.

123 Respect your children's privacy. Knock before entering their room.

124 Learn to listen.
Opportunity sometimes
knocks very softly.

125   Know how to change a tire.

126   Know how to tie a bow tie.

127   Wear audacious underwear under the most solemn business attire.

128   Remember people's names.

129   Introduce yourself to the manager where you bank. It's important that he or she knows you personally.

130   Learn the capitals of the states.

131   Visit Washington, D.C., and do the tourist bit.

132 Leave the toilet seat in the down position.

133 When someone is relating an important event that's happened to them, don't try to top them with a story of your own. Let them have the stage.

134 Have crooked teeth straightened.

135 Have dull-colored teeth whitened.

136 Keep your watch five minutes fast.

137 Learn Spanish. In a few years, more than thirty-five percent of all Americans will speak it as their first language.

138 Never deprive someone of hope; it might be all they have.

139   When starting out, don't worry about not having enough money. Limited funds are a blessing, not a curse. Nothing encourages creative thinking in quite the same way.

140   Give yourself an hour to cool off before responding to someone who has provoked you. If it involves something really important, give yourself overnight.

141   Keep a flashlight and extra batteries under the bed and in the glove box of your car.

142   Don't buy cheap tools. Craftsman tools from Sears are among the best.

143 Pay your bills on time.

144 Join a slow-pitch softball league.

145 Take someone bowling.

146 When playing games with children, let them win.

147 Turn off the television at dinner time.

148 Learn to handle a pistol and rifle safely.

149 Skip one meal a week and give what you would have spent to a street person.

150 Sing in a choir.

151 Get acquainted with a good lawyer, accountant, and plumber.

152 Fly Old Glory on the Fourth of July.

153 Stand at attention and put your hand over your heart when singing the national anthem.

154 Resist the temptation to put a cute message on your answering machine.

155 Have a will and tell your next-of-kin where it is.

156 Strive for excellence, not perfection.

157 Take time to smell the roses.

158 Pray not for things, but for wisdom and courage.

159 Be tough minded but tenderhearted.

160 Use seat belts.

161 Have regular medical and dental checkups.

162 Keep your desk and work area neat.

163 Take an overnight train trip and sleep in a Pullman.

164 Be punctual and insist on it in others.

165 Don't scrimp in order to leave money to your children.

166 Don't waste time responding to your critics.

167 Avoid negative people.

168 Resist telling people how something should be done. Instead, tell them *what* needs to be done. They will often surprise you with creative solutions.

169 Be original.

170 Be neat.

171 Never give up on what you really want to do. The person with big dreams is more powerful than one with all the facts.

172 Be kinder than necessary.

173 Be suspicious of all politicians.

174 Encourage your children to have a part-time job after the age of sixteen.

175 Give people a second chance, but not a third.

176 Read carefully anything that requires your signature. Remember the big print giveth and the small print taketh away.

177 Learn to recognize the inconsequential; then ignore it.

178 Do battle against prejudice and discrimination wherever you find it.

179   Never take action when you're angry.

180   Be your wife's best friend.

181   Be romantic.

182   Let people know what you stand for—and what you won't stand for.

183   Don't quit a job until you've lined up another.

184   Never criticize the person who signs your paycheck. If you are unhappy with your job, resign.

185   Wear out, don't rust out.

186 Become the most positive
and enthusiastic person
you know.

187 Be insatiably curious. Ask "why" a lot.

188 Measure people by the size of their hearts, not the size of their bank accounts.

189 Have good posture. Enter a room with purpose and confidence.

190 Don't worry that you can't give your kids the best of everything. Give them *your* very best.

191 Drink low fat milk.

192 Use less salt.

193 Eat less red meat.

194 Learn how to fix a leaky faucet and toilet.

195 Determine the quality of a neighborhood by the manners of the people living there.

196 Surprise a new neighbor with one of your favorite homemade dishes—and include the recipe.

197 Don't forget, a person's greatest emotional need is to feel appreciated.

198 Feed a stranger's expired parking meter.

199 Park at the back of the lot at shopping centers. The walk is good exercise.

200 Don't watch violent television shows, and don't buy the products that sponsor them.

201 Don't carry a grudge.

202 Show respect for all living things.

203 Return borrowed vehicles with the gas tank full.

204 Choose work that is in harmony with your values.

205 Loosen up. Relax. Except for rare life-and-death matters, nothing is as important as it first seems.

206 Swing for the fence.

207 Commit yourself
to constant
self-improvement.

208 Give your best to your employer. It's one of the best investments you can make.

209 Attend high school art shows, and always buy something.

210 Observe the speed limit.

211 Take your dog to obedience school. You'll both learn a lot.

212 Don't waste time grieving over past mistakes. Learn from them and move on.

213 When complimented, a sincere "thank you" is the only response required.

214 Don't plan a long evening on a blind date. A lunch date is perfect. If things don't work out, both of you have wasted only an hour.

215 Don't discuss business in elevators. You never know who may overhear you.

216 Be a good loser.

217 Be a good winner.

218 Never go grocery shopping when you're hungry. You'll buy too much.

219 Spend less time worrying *who's* right, and more time deciding *what's* right.

220 # Don't major in minor things.

221 Don't allow the phone to interrupt important moments. It's there for your convenience, not the caller's.

222 Think twice before burdening a friend with a secret.

223 Praise in public.

224 Criticize in private.

225 When someone hugs you, let them be the first to let go.

226 Resist giving advice concerning matrimony, finances, or hair styles.

227 Never tell anyone they look tired or depressed.

228 Have impeccable manners.

229 Never pay for work before it's completed.

230 Keep good company.

231 Keep a daily journal.

232 Keep your promises.

233 Avoid any church that has cushions on the pews and is considering building a gymnasium.

234 Teach your children the value of money and the importance of saving.

235 Be willing to lose a battle in order to win the war.

236 Don't be deceived by first impressions.

237 Seek out the good in people.

238 Don't encourage rude or inattentive service by tipping the standard amount.

239 Watch the movie *It's a Wonderful Life* every Christmas.

240 Drink eight glasses of water every day.

241 Respect tradition.

242 Never cut
what can be untied.

243 Be cautious about lending money to friends. You might lose both.

244 Never waste an opportunity to tell good employees how much they mean to the company.

245 Buy a bird feeder and hang it so that you can see it from your kitchen window.

246 Wave at children on school buses.

247 Show respect for others' time. Call whenever you're going to be more than ten minutes late for an appointment.

248   Tape record your parents' memories of how they met and their first years of marriage.

249   Hire people smarter than you.

250   Be modest. A lot was accomplished before you were born.

251   Take good care of those you love.

252   Keep it simple.

253   Purchase gas from the neighborhood gas station even if it costs more. Next winter when it's six degrees and your car won't start, you'll be glad they know you.

254 Learn to show enthusiasm, even when you don't feel like it.

255 Learn to show cheerfulness, even when you don't feel like it.

256 Don't jaywalk.

257 Never ask a lawyer or accountant for business advice. They are trained to find problems, not solutions.

258 Avoid like the plague any lawsuit.

259 Take family vacations whether you can afford them or not. The memories will be priceless.

260 Every day show your family how much you love them with your words, with your touch, and with your thoughtfulness.

261 Don't gossip.

262 Don't discuss salaries.

263 Don't nag.

264 Don't gamble.

265 Beware of the person who has nothing to lose.

266 Lie on your back and look at the stars.

267 Don't leave car keys in the ignition.

268 When meeting someone for the first time, resist asking what they do for a living. Enjoy their company without attaching any labels.

269 Don't whine.

270 Arrive at work early and stay beyond quitting time.

271 When facing a difficult task, act as though it is impossible to fail. If you're going after Moby Dick, take along the tarter sauce.

272 Change air conditioner filters every three months.

273 Leave everything a little better than you found it.

274 Remember that overnight success usually takes about fifteen years.

275 Cut out complimentary newspaper articles about people you know and mail the articles to them with notes of congratulations.

276 Patronize local merchants even if it costs a bit more.

277 Fill your gas tank when it falls below one-quarter full.

278 Never snap your fingers to get someone's attention. It's rude.

279 Don't expect money to bring you happiness.

280 No matter how dire the situation, keep your cool.

281 When paying cash, ask for a discount.

282 Find a good tailor.

283 Don't use a toothpick in public.

284 Never underestimate your power to change yourself.

285 Never overestimate your power to change others.

286 Practice empathy. Try to see things from other people's point of view.

287 Promise big. Deliver big.

288 Discipline yourself to save money. It's essential to success.

289 Find some other way of proving your manhood than by shooting defenseless animals and birds.

290 Remember the deal's not done until the check has cleared the bank.

291 Don't burn bridges. You'll be surprised how many times you have to cross the same river.

292 Don't spread yourself too thin. Learn to say *no* politely and quickly.

293 Keep overhead low.

294 Keep expectations high.

295 Remember that a successful marriage depends on two things: (1) finding the right person and (2) being the right person.

296 See problems as opportunities for growth and self-mastery.

297 Don't believe people when they ask you to be honest with them.

298 Get and stay in shape.

299 Accept pain and disappointment as part of life.

300 Don't expect life to be fair.

301 Become an expert in time management.

302 Lock your car even if it's parked in your own driveway.

303 Never go to bed with dirty dishes in the sink.

304 Learn to handle a handsaw and a hammer.

305 Compliment the meal when you're a guest in someone's home.

306 Judge your success by the degree that you're enjoying peace, health, and love.

307 Take a nap on Sunday afternoons.

308 Make the bed when you're an overnight visitor in someone's home.

309 Contribute five percent of your income to charity.

310 Don't leave a ring in the bathtub.

311 When tempted to criticize your parents, spouse, or children, bite your tongue.

312 Never underestimate the power of love.

313 Never underestimate the power of forgiveness.

314 Don't waste time playing cards.

315 Don't bore people with your problems. When someone asks you how you feel—say, "Terrific, never better." When they ask, "How's business?" reply, "Excellent, and getting better every day."

316 Learn to disagree without being disagreeable.

317 Be tactful. Never alienate anyone on purpose.

318 Hear both sides before judging.

319 Be courteous to everyone.

320 Wave to crosswalk patrol mothers.

321 Refrain from envy. It's the source of much unhappiness.

322 Don't say you don't have enough time. You have exactly the same number of hours per day that were given to Helen Keller, Pasteur, Michaelangelo, Mother Teresa, Leonardo da Vinci, Thomas Jefferson, and Albert Einstein.

323 When there's no time for a full work-out, do push-ups.

324 Don't delay acting on a good idea. Chances are someone else has just thought of it, too. Success comes to the one who acts first.

325 Be wary of people who tell you how honest they are.

326 Remember that winners do what losers don't want to do.

327 Rekindle old friendships.

328 When traveling, put a card in your wallet with your name, home phone, the phone number of a friend or close relative, important medical information, plus the phone number of the hotel or motel where you're staying.

329 Every so often push your luck.

330 Live your life as an
exclamation, not an
explanation.

331 When you arrive at your job in the morning, let the first thing you say brighten everyone's day.

332 Seek opportunity, not security. A boat in a harbor is safe, but in time its bottom will rot out.

333 Instead of using the words, *if only,* try substituting the words, *next time.*

334 Instead of using the word *problem,* try substituting the word *opportunity.*

335 Reread your favorite book.

336 Live your life so that your epitaph could read, "No regrets."

337   Install smoke detectors in your home.

338   Get your next pet from the animal shelter.

339   Don't think a higher price always means higher quality.

340   Don't be fooled. If something sounds too good to be true, it probably is.

341   When renting a car for a couple of days, splurge and get the big Lincoln.

342   Regarding furniture and clothes: if you think you'll be using them five years or longer, buy the best you can afford.

343 Never walk out on a quarrel with your wife.

344 Patronize drug stores with soda fountains.

345 Try everything offered by supermarket food demonstrators.

346 Be bold and courageous. When you look back on your life, you'll regret the things you didn't do more than the ones you did.

347 Remember the three most important things when buying a home: location, location, location.

348 Just for fun, attend a small town Fourth of July celebration.

349 Never waste an
opportunity to tell
someone you love them.

350 Own a good dictionary.

351 Own a good thesaurus.

352 Keep valuable papers in a bank lockbox.

353 Go through all your old photographs. Select ten and tape them to your kitchen cabinets. Change them every thirty days.

354 Be there when people need you.

355 Let your representatives in Washington know how you feel. Call (202) 225-3121 for the House and (202) 224-3121 for the Senate. An operator will connect you to the right office.

356 To explain a romantic break-up, simply say, "It was all my fault."

357 Evaluate yourself by your own standards, not someone else's.

358 Be decisive even if it means you'll sometimes be wrong.

359 Don't let anyone talk you out of pursuing what you know to be a great idea.

360 Be prepared to lose once in a while.

361 Don't flush urinals with your hand—use your elbow.

362   Know when to keep silent.

363   Know when to speak up.

364   Every day look for some small way to improve your marriage.

365   Every day look for some small way to improve the way you do your job.

366   Acquire things the old-fashioned way: Save for them and pay cash.

367   Remember no one makes it alone. Have a grateful heart and be quick to acknowledge those who help you.

368 Never eat the last cookie.

369 Read *Leadership Is an Art* by Max DePree (Dell, 1989).

370 Do business with those who do business with you.

371 Just to see how it feels, for the next twenty-four hours refrain from criticizing anybody or anything.

372 Give your clients your enthusiastic best.

373 Save an evening a week for just you and your wife.

374 Take charge of your attitude. Don't let someone else choose it for you.

375 Let your children overhear you saying complimentary things about them to other adults.

376 Work hard to create in your children a good self-image. It's the most important thing you can do to insure their success.

377 Carry jumper cables in your car.

378 Get all repair estimates in writing.

379 Forget committees. New, noble, world-changing ideas always come from one person working alone.

380 Pay attention to the details.

381 Be a self-starter.

382 Be loyal.

383 Understand that happiness is not based on possessions, power, or prestige, but on relationships with people you love and respect.

384 Never give a loved one a gift that suggests they need improvement.

385 Compliment even small improvements.

386 Turn off the tap when brushing your teeth.

387 Wear expensive shoes, belts, and ties, but buy them on sale.

388 When undecided about what color to paint a room, choose antique white.

389 Carry stamps in your wallet. You never know when you'll discover the perfect card for a friend or loved one.

390 Street musicians are a treasure. Stop for a moment and listen; then leave a small donation.

391 When faced with a serious health problem, get at least three medical opinions.

392 Support equal pay for equal work.

393 Pay your fair share.

394 Learn how to use the internet.

395 Remain open, flexible, curious.

396 Never give anyone a fruitcake.

397 Never acquire just one kitten. Two are a lot more fun and no more trouble.

398 Start meetings on time regardless of who's missing.

399 Stay out of nightclubs.

400 Focus on making things better, not bigger.

401 Don't ever watch hot dogs or sausage being made.

402 Begin each day with your favorite music.

403 Visit your city's night court on a Saturday night.

404 Don't be intimidated by doctors and nurses. Even when you're in the hospital, it's still your body.

405 Read hospital bills carefully. It's reported that 89% contain errors—in favor of the hospital.

406 Send a lot of Valentine cards. Sign them, "Someone who thinks you're terrific."

407 When attending meetings, sit down front.

408 Every once in a while, take the scenic route.

409 Don't let your possessions possess you.

410 Wage war against littering.

411 Cut your own firewood.

412 When you and your wife have a disagreement, regardless of who's wrong, apologize. Say, "I'm sorry I upset you. Would you forgive me?" These are healing, magical words.

413 Be enthusiastic about the success of others.

414 Don't flaunt your success, but don't apologize for it either.

415 After experiencing inferior service, food, or products, bring it to the attention of the person in charge. Good managers will appreciate knowing.

416 Don't procrastinate. Do what needs doing when it needs to be done.

417 Read to your children.

418 Sing to your children.

419 Listen to your children.

420 Take care of your reputation. It's your most valuable asset.

421 Get your priorities straight. No one ever said on his death bed, "Gee, if I'd only spent more time at the office."

422 Turn on your headlights when it begins to rain.

423 Don't tailgate.

424 Sign and carry your organ donor card.

425 Don't allow self-pity. The moment this emotion strikes, do something nice for someone less fortunate than you.

426 Improve your performance by improving your attitude.

427 Share the credit.

428 Don't accept "good enough" as good enough.

429 Do more than is expected.

430 Go to a county fair and check out the 4-H Club exhibits. It will renew your faith in the younger generation.

431 Select a doctor your own age so that you can grow old together.

432 Make a list of twenty-five things you want to experience before you die. Carry it in your wallet and refer to it often.

433 Use club soda as an emergency spot remover.

434 Have a friend who owns a truck.

435 At the movies, buy Junior Mints and sprinkle them on your popcorn.

436 Have some knowledge of three religions other than your own.

437 Answer the phone with enthusiasm and energy in your voice.

438 Change your car's oil and filter every three thousand miles regardless of what the owner's manual recommends.

439 Every person that you meet knows something you don't; learn from them.

440 Tape record your parents' laughter.

441 Never put a candy dish next to the phone.

442 When meeting someone you don't know well, extend your hand and give them your name. Never assume they remember you even if you've met them before.

443 Do it right the first time.

444 Laugh a lot. A good sense of humor cures almost all of life's ills.

445 Never underestimate the
power of a kind word
or deed.

446 Don't undertip the waiter just because the food is bad; he didn't cook it.

447 Conduct family fire drills. Be sure everyone knows what to do in case the house catches fire.

448 Don't be afraid to say, "I don't know."

449 Don't be afraid to say, "I made a mistake."

450 Don't be afraid to say, "I need help."

451 Don't be afraid to say, "I'm sorry."

452 Show respect for everyone who works for a living, regardless of how trivial their job.

453   Never compromise your integrity.

454   Keep a note pad and pencil on your bedside table. Million-dollar ideas sometimes strike at 3 A.M.

455   Read the Sunday *New York Times* to keep informed.

456   Send your loved one flowers. Think of a reason later.

457   Get organized. If you don't know where to start, read Stephanie Winston's *Getting Organized* (Warner Books, 1978).

458 Attend your children's athletic contests, plays, and recitals.

459 When you find a job that's ideal, take it regardless of the pay. If you've got what it takes, your salary will soon reflect your value to the company.

460 Look for opportunities to make people feel important.

461 Be open to new ideas.

462 Don't miss the magic of the moment by focusing on what's to come.

463 Don't use time or words carelessly. Neither can be retrieved.

464 When a child falls and skins a knee or elbow, always show concern; then take the time to "kiss it and make it well."

465 When talking to the press, remember they always have the last word.

466 Set short-term and long-term goals.

467 When planning a trip abroad, read about the places you'll visit before you go or, better yet, rent a travel video.

468 Don't rain on other people's parades.

469 Stand when greeting a visitor to your office.

470 Don't interrupt.

471 Before leaving to meet a flight, call the airline first to be sure it's on time.

472 Enjoy real maple syrup.

473 Don't be rushed into making an important decision. People will understand if you say, "I'd like a little more time to think it over. Can I get back to you tomorrow?"

474 Be prepared. You never get a second chance to make a good first impression.

475 Give thanks before every meal.

476 Don't expect others to listen to your advice and ignore your example.

477 Go the distance. When you accept a task, finish it.

478 Don't insist on running someone else's life.

479 Decide to get up thirty minutes earlier. Do this for a year, and you will add seven and one-half days to your waking world.

480 Get into the habit of putting your billfold and car keys in the same place when entering your home.

481 Watch for big problems. They disguise big opportunities.

482 Learn a card trick.

483 Steer clear of restaurants that rotate.

484 Give people the benefit of the doubt.

485 Never admit at work that you're tired, angry, or bored.

486 Respond promptly to R.S.V.P. invitations. If there's a phone number, call; if not, write a note.

487 Take a kid to the zoo.

488 Make someone's day by paying the toll for the person in the car behind you.

489   Don't make the same mistake twice.

490   Don't drive on slick tires.

491   Keep an extra key hidden somewhere on your car in case you lock yourself out.

492   Put an insulation blanket around your hot water heater to conserve energy.

493   Save ten percent of what you earn.

494   Never discuss money with people who have much more or much less than you.

495   Never buy a beige car.

496 Don't be called out on strikes. Go down swinging.

497 Never buy something you don't need just because it's on sale.

498 Question your goals by asking, "Will this help me become my very best?"

499 Cherish your children for what they are, not for what you'd like them to be.

500 When negotiating your salary, think of what you want; then ask for ten percent more.

501 Keep several irons in the fire.

502 After you've worked hard to get what you want, take the time to enjoy it.

503 Be alert for opportunities to show praise and appreciation.

504 Commit yourself to quality.

505 Be a leader: Remember the lead sled dog is the only one with a decent view.

506 Never underestimate the power of words to heal and reconcile relationships.

507 Your mind can only hold one thought at a time. Make it a positive and constructive one.

508 Become someone's hero.

509 Marry only for love.

510 Count your blessings.

511 Call your mother.

VOLUME TWO

512 Believe in love at first sight.

513 Never laugh at anyone's dreams.

514 Overpay good baby sitters.

515 Never refuse jury duty. It is your civic responsibility, and you'll learn a lot.

516 Love deeply and passionately. You might get hurt, but it's the only way to live life completely.

517 Carry Handi-Wipes in your glove compartment.

518 Never apologize for being early for an appointment.

519 Open the car door for your wife and always help her with her coat.

520 When reconvening after a conference break, choose a chair in a different part of the room.

521 Read the ten books nominated each year for the ABBY Award.

522 Rake a big pile of leaves every fall and jump in it with someone you love.

523 Create a little signal only your wife knows so that you can show her you love her across a crowded room.

524 Accept a breath mint if someone offers you one.

525 When you feel terrific, notify your face.

526 Discipline with a gentle hand.

527 Volunteer. Sometimes the jobs no one wants conceal big opportunities.

528 Never drive while holding a cup of hot coffee between your knees.

529 Use a travel agent. It costs no more and saves time and effort.

530 Never be the first to break a family tradition.

531 Have a professional photo of yourself made.
Update it every three years.

532 Never miss an opportunity to ride a roller
coaster.

533 Never miss an opportunity to have someone
rub your back.

534 Never miss an opportunity to sleep on a
screened-in porch.

535 Remember the advice of our friend Ken Beck:
When you see a box turtle crossing the road,
stop and put it safely on the other side.

536 Sign all warranty cards and mail them in promptly.

537 Drive as you wish your kids would. Never speed or drive recklessly with children in the car.

538 Park next to the end curb in parking lots. Your car doors will have half the chance of getting dented.

539 Ask about a store's return policy when you purchase an item that costs more than $50.

540 When you go to borrow money, dress as if you have plenty of it.

541 Keep a diary of your accomplishments at work. Then when you ask for a raise, you'll have the information you need to back it up.

542 Never sign contracts with blank spaces.

543 In disagreements, fight fairly. No name calling.

544 Never take the last piece of fried chicken.

545 Never pick up anything off the floor of a cab.

546 Don't judge people by their relatives.

547 Eat a piece of chocolate to cure bad breath from onions or garlic.

548 Seize every opportunity for additional training in your job.

549 Put your address inside your luggage as well as on the outside.

550 Never give your credit card number over the phone if you didn't place the call.

551 Remember that everyone you meet is afraid of something, loves something, and has lost something.

552 Check hotel bills carefully, especially the charges for local and long-distance calls.

553 Talk slow
but think quick.

554   When traveling, leave the good jewelry at home.

555   When someone asks you a question you don't want to answer, smile and ask, "Why do you want to know?"

556   Don't admire people for their wealth but for the creative and generous ways they put it to use.

557   Take along two big safety pins when you travel so that you can pin the drapes shut in your motel room.

558   Never leave the kitchen when something's boiling on the stove.

559   Never betray a confidence.

560   Never claim a victory prematurely.

561   Say "bless you" when you hear someone sneeze.

562   Remember that just the moment you say, "I give up," someone else seeing the same situation is saying, "My, what a great opportunity."

563   Tour the main branch of the public library on Fifth Avenue the next time you are in New York City. Unforgettable.

564   Never give anybody a fondue set or anything painted avocado green.

565   Make the punishment fit the crime.

566   Don't let your family get so busy that you don't sit down to at least one meal a day together.

567   Remember the three Rs: Respect for self; Respect for others; Responsibility for all your actions.

568   Carry your own alarm clock when traveling. Hotel wake-up calls are sometimes unreliable.

569   When you lose, don't lose the lesson.

570   Take along a small gift for the host or hostess when you're a dinner guest. A book is a good choice.

571 Keep the porch light on until all the family is in for the night.

572 Plant zucchini only if you have lots of friends.

573 Don't overlook life's small joys while searching for the big ones.

574 Keep a well-stocked first-aid kit in your car and at home.

575 Never be photographed with a cocktail glass in your hand.

576 Order a seed catalog. Read it on the day of the first snowfall.

577   Don't let a little dispute injure a great friendship.

578   Don't marry a woman who picks at her food.

579   Pack a compass and the Nature Company's pocket survival tool when hiking in unfamiliar territory.

580   When lost or in distress, signal in "threes"— three shouts, three gunshots, or three horn blasts.

581   Don't be surprised to discover that luck favors those who are prepared.

582   When asked to play the piano, do it without complaining or making excuses.

583   Read a book about beekeeping.

584   Subscribe to *Consumer Reports* magazine.

585   Don't expect your love alone to make a neat person out of a messy one.

586   Take off the convention badge as soon as you leave the convention hall.

587   Look for ways to make your boss look good.

588   Every so often, invite the person in line behind you to go ahead of you.

589   Carry a small pocket knife.

590 Remember that the person who steals an egg will steal a chicken.

591 Meet regularly with someone who holds vastly different views than you.

592 Be the first to fight for a just cause.

593 When you have the choice of two exciting things, choose the one you haven't tried.

594 Remember that no time spent with your children is ever wasted.

595 Remember that no time is ever wasted that makes two people better friends.

596 Give people more than they expect and do it cheerfully.

597 Don't go looking for trouble.

598 Don't buy someone else's trouble.

599 Avoid approaching horses and restaurants from the rear.

600 There are people who will always come up with reasons why you can't do what you want to do. Ignore them.

601 If you need to bring in a business partner, make sure your partner brings along some money.

602 Never say anything uncomplimentary about another person's dog.

603 If you have trouble with a company's products or services, go to the top. Write the president, then follow up with a phone call.

604 Don't ride in a car if the driver has been drinking.

605 Call the Better Business Bureau if you're not sure about a business' reputation.

606 Think twice before accepting the lowest bid.

607 When boarding a bus, say "hello" to the driver. Say "thank you" when you get off.

608 Never give a gift that's not beautifully wrapped.

609 Check to see if your regular car insurance covers you when you rent a car. The insurance offered by car rental companies is expensive.

610 When in doubt about what art to put on a wall, choose a framed black-and-white photo by Ansel Adams.

611 When uncertain what to wear, a blue blazer, worn with gray wool slacks, a white shirt, and a red-and-blue striped silk tie, is almost always appropriate.

612 Write a short note inside the front cover when giving a book as a gift.

613 Make the rules for your children clear, fair, and consistent.

614 Don't think expensive equipment will make up for lack of talent or practice.

615 Learn to say "I love you" in French, Italian, and Swedish.

616 On a clear night, look for Orion's Belt and think of your mother. It's her favorite constellation.

617 Memorize your favorite love poem.

618 Ask anyone giving you directions to repeat them at least twice.

619 When you are totally exhausted but have to keep going, wash your face and hands and put on clean socks and a clean shirt. You will feel remarkably refreshed.

620 Make allowances for your friends' imperfections as readily as you do for your own.

621 Pay your bills on time. If you can't, write your creditors a letter describing your situation. Send them something every month, even if it's only five dollars.

622 Steer clear of any place with a Ladies Welcome sign in the window.

623 When you realize you've made a mistake, take immediate steps to correct it.

624 Be ruthlessly realistic when it comes to your finances.

625 Smile when picking up the phone. The caller will hear it in your voice.

626 Ask yourself if you would feel comfortable giving your two best friends a key to your house. If not, look for some new best friends.

627 Set high goals for your employees and help them attain them.

628   Never miss a chance to dance with your wife.

629   Do your homework and know your facts, but remember it's passion that persuades.

630   Don't waste time trying to appreciate music you dislike. Spend the time with music you love.

631   Learn how to make tapioca pudding and peanut brittle in the microwave.

632   Set aside your dreams for your children and help them attain their own dreams.

633   Dress a little better than your clients but not as well as your boss.

634 Always put something in the collection plate.

635 When concluding a business deal and the other person suggests working out the details later, say, "I understand, but I would like to settle the entire matter right now." Don't move from the table until you do.

636 Do the right thing, regardless of what others think.

637 Wear a shirt and tie to job interviews, even for a job unloading boxcars.

638 Learn to save on even the most modest salary. If you do, you're almost assured of financial success.

639 Take the stairs when it's four flights or less.

640 Judge people from where they stand, not from where you stand.

641 When shaking a woman's hand, squeeze it no harder than she squeezes yours.

642 Be open and accessible. The next person you meet could become your best friend.

643 Never wash a car, mow a yard, or select a Christmas tree after dark.

644 Life will sometimes hand you a magical moment. Savor it.

645 Never threaten if you don't intend to back it up.

646 Buy a used car with the same caution a naked man uses to climb a barbed-wire fence.

647 Hold yourself to the highest standards.

648 Buy the big bottle of Tabasco.

649 Don't confuse comfort with happiness.

650 Don't confuse wealth with success.

651 Be the first to forgive.

652 Make a habit of reading something inspiring and cheerful just before going to sleep.

653 When talking to your doctor, don't let him or her interrupt or end the session early. It's your body and your money. Stay until all your questions are answered to your satisfaction.

654 Whenever you take something back for an exchange or refund, wear a coat and tie.

655 Check for toilet paper *before* sitting down.

656 Don't stop the parade to pick up a dime.

657 Marry a woman you love to talk to. As you get older, her conversational skills will be as important as any other.

658 Turn enemies into friends by doing something nice for them.

659 If you work for an organization that makes its decisions by committee, make darn sure you're on the committee.

660 When hiring, give special consideration to a man who is an Eagle Scout and a woman who has received the Girl Scout Gold Award.

661 Ask for double prints when you have film processed. Send the extras to the people in the photos.

662 If you want to do something and you feel in your bones that it's the right thing to do, do it. Intuition is often as important as the facts.

663 Remember that a person who is foolish with money is foolish in other ways too.

664 Don't cut corners.

665 Learn to bake bread.

666 Everyone loves praise. Look hard for ways to give it to them.

667 Be an original. If that means being a little eccentric, so be it.

668 Pay as much attention to the things that are working positively in your life as you do to those that are giving you trouble.

669 Spend some time alone.

670 Everybody deserves a birthday cake. Never celebrate a birthday without one.

671 Open your arms to change, but don't let go of your values.

672 When it comes to worrying or painting a picture, know when to stop.

673 Don't expect anyone to know what you want for Christmas if you don't tell them.

674 Before taking a long trip, fill your tank and empty your bladder.

675 Be as friendly to the janitor as you are to the chairman of the board.

676 Mind your own business.

677 When taking a woman home, make sure she's safely inside her house before you leave.

678 Live with your new pet several days before you name it. The right name will come to you.

679 Every year celebrate the day you and your wife had your first date.

680 Treat your employees with the same respect you give your clients.

681 Be quick to take advantage
of an advantage.

682 Slow down. I mean *really* slow down in school zones.

683 Allow your children to face the consequences of their actions.

684 Don't expect the best gifts to come wrapped in pretty paper.

685 When a good man or woman runs for political office, support him or her with your time and money.

686 When you need professional advice, get it from professionals, not from your friends.

687 You may be fortunate and make a lot of money, but be sure your work involves something that enriches your spirit as well as your bank account.

688 Remember that silence is sometimes the best answer.

689 Don't buy a cheap mattress.

690 Don't think you can relax your way to happiness. Happiness comes as a result of *doing*.

691 Don't dismiss a good idea simply because you don't like the source.

692   Pay for a poor child to go to summer camp.

693   Choose a church that sings joyful music.

694   What you must do, do cheerfully.

695   Don't waste time waiting for inspiration. Begin, and inspiration will find you.

696   When you say, "I love you," mean it.

697   When you say, "I'm sorry," look the person in the eye.

698   Be engaged at least six months before you get married.

699 Don't believe all you hear,
spend all you have,
or sleep all you want.

700 Conduct yourself in such a way that your high school would want you to address the graduating seniors.

701 Win without boasting.

702 Lose without excuses.

703 Watch your attitude. It's the first thing people notice about you.

704 Choose the apartment on the top floor.

705 Ask someone you'd like to know better to list five people he would most like to meet. It will tell you a lot about him.

706 Pack a light bathrobe on overnight trips. Take your pillow, too.

707 Don't be a person who says, "Ready, fire, aim."

708 Don't be a person who says, "Ready, aim, aim, aim."

709 Deadlines are important. Meet them.

710 When you find someone doing small things well, put him or her in charge of bigger things.

711 Read more books.

712 Watch less TV.

713 # When opportunity knocks, invite it to stay for dinner.

714 Remember that a good price is not necessarily what an object is marked, but what it is worth to you.

715 When a waitress or waiter provides exceptional service, leave a generous tip, plus a short note like, "Thanks for the wonderful service. You made our meal a special experience."

716 Remember that the more you know, the less you fear.

717 When a friend or loved one becomes ill, remember that hope and positive thinking are strong medicines.

718 Buy three best-selling children's books. Read them and then give them to a youngster.

719 Introduce yourself to your neighbors as soon as you move into a new neighborhood.

720 Remove your sunglasses when you talk to someone.

721 When you find something you really want, don't let a few dollars keep you from getting it.

722 Become your children's best teacher and coach.

723 Buy ladders, extension cords, and garden hoses longer than you think you'll need.

724   Some things need doing better than they've ever been done before. Some just need doing. Others don't need doing at all. Know which is which.

725   Don't confuse mere inconveniences with real problems.

726   When asked to pray in public, be quick about it.

727   Show extra respect for people whose jobs put dirt under their fingernails.

728   Hold your child's hand every chance you get. The time will come all too soon when he or she won't let you.

729 Remember that
a good example
is the best sermon.

730 When you carve the Thanksgiving turkey, give the first piece to the person who prepared it.

731 Live a good, honorable life. Then when you get older and think back, you'll get to enjoy it a second time.

732 Wipe off the sticky honey jar before putting it back on the shelf.

733 Purchase one piece of original art each year, even if it's just a small painting by a high school student.

734 Learn to juggle.

735 Volunteer to work a few hours each month in a soup kitchen.

736 Don't think people at the top of their professions have all the answers. They don't.

737 Learn to make great spaghetti sauce. Your mother's recipe is the best.

738 If you're treated unfairly by an airline, contact the Consumer Affairs Office of the Department of Transportation at (202) 366-2220.

739 Don't carry expensive luggage. It's a tip-off to thieves that expensive items may be inside.

740　Get a car with a sun roof.

741　When traveling by plane, don't pack valuables or important papers in your suitcase. Carry them on board with you.

742　Keep your private thoughts private.

743　Put your jacket around your girlfriend on a chilly evening.

744　Introduce yourself to someone you would like to meet by smiling and saying, "My name is Adam Brown. I haven't had the pleasure of meeting you."

745 Once every couple of months enjoy a four-course meal—but eat each course at a different restaurant.

746 Be humble and polite, but don't let anyone push you around.

747 Put the strap around your neck before looking through binoculars.

748 Do 100 push-ups every day: 50 in the morning and 50 in the evening.

749 Wear safety glasses when operating a Weed Eater or power saw.

750 Wrap a couple of thick rubber bands around your wallet when you're fishing or hiking. This will prevent it from slipping out of your pocket.

751 Don't expect bankers to come to your aid in a crunch.

752 Be advised that when negotiating, if you don't get it in writing, you probably won't get it.

753 Don't do business with anyone who has a history of suing people.

754 Every so often let your spirit of adventure triumph over your good sense.

755 # Trust in God,
but lock your car.

756 Use a favorite picture of a loved one as a bookmark.

757 Never lose your nerve, your temper, or your car keys.

758 Surprise an old friend with a phone call.

759 Get involved at your child's school.

760 Champion your wife. Be her best friend and biggest fan.

761 Add to your children's private library by giving them a hardback copy of one of the classics every birthday. Begin with their first birthday.

762 Carry a list of your wife's important sizes in your wallet.

763 Don't open credit card bills on the weekend.

764 Mind the store. No one cares about your business the way you do.

765 When you are a dinner guest, take a second helping if it's offered, but never a third.

766 Never say anything uncomplimentary about your wife or children in the presence of others.

767 Before going to bed on Christmas Eve, join hands with your family and sing "Silent Night."

768 Don't say no until you've heard the whole story.

769 Don't accept unacceptable behavior.

770 Never put the car in "drive" until all passengers have buckled up.

771 When eating at a restaurant that features foreign food, don't order anything you can fix at home.

772 Send your mother-in-law flowers on your wife's birthday.

773 When giving a speech, concentrate on what you can give the audience, not what you can get from them.

774 Write your pastor a note and tell him how much he means to you.

775 Write your favorite author a note of appreciation.

776 Apologize immediately when you lose your temper, especially to children.

777 When you're uncertain of what you should pay someone, ask, "What do you think is fair?" You'll almost always get a reasonable answer.

778 When you know that someone has gone to a lot of trouble to get dressed up, tell them they look terrific!

779 # Don't let weeds grow around your dreams.

780 Buy your fiancé the nicest diamond engagement ring you can afford.

781 Don't be so concerned with your rights that you forget your manners.

782 A loving atmosphere in your home is so important. Do all you can to create a tranquil, harmonious home.

783 Remember that almost everything looks better after a good night's sleep.

784 Avoid using the word *impacted* unless you are describing wisdom teeth.

785 When you tell a child to do something, don't follow it with, "Okay?" Ask instead, "Do you understand?"

786 In disagreements with loved ones, deal with the current situation. Don't bring up the past.

787 Leave a quarter where a child can find it.

788 Read William Safire's *Lend Me Your Ears*, a collection of the world's great speeches (W. W. Norton & Co., 1992).

789 Keep a separate shaving kit packed just for traveling.

790 Remember that *how* you say something is as important as *what* you say.

791 Every so often watch *Sesame Street*.

792 Read between the lines.

793 Get to garage sales early. The good stuff is usually gone by 8:00 a.m.

794 Stop and watch stonemasons at work.

795 Stop and watch a farmer plowing a field.

796 If your town has a baseball team, attend the season opener.

797 When you see visitors taking pictures of each other, offer to take a picture of them together.

798 Don't think you can fill an emptiness in your heart with money.

799 Never apologize for extreme measures when defending your values, your health, or your family's safety.

800 Use a camcorder to videotape the contents of your home for insurance purposes. Don't forget closets and drawers. Keep the tape in your bank safe-deposit box.

801 Become famous for finishing important, difficult tasks.

802 Never sell your teddy bear, letter sweater, or high school yearbooks at a garage sale. You'll regret it later.

803 Buy a new tie to wear to your wedding rehearsal dinner. Wear it only once. Keep it forever.

804 When you're lost, admit it, and ask for directions.

805 Never buy just one roll of toilet paper, one roll of film, or one jar of peanut butter. Get two.

806 Don't take good friends, good health, or a good marriage for granted.

807 Place a note reading "Your license number has been reported to the police" on the windshield of a car illegally parked in a handicapped space.

808 Do a good job because you want to, not because you have to. This puts you in charge instead of your boss.

809 Remember that the shortest way to get anywhere is to have good company traveling with you.

810 Never type a love letter. Use a fountain pen.

811 Never buy a chair or sofa without first sitting on it for several minutes.

812 Don't be thin-skinned. Take criticism as well as praise with equal grace.

813 At the end of your days, be leaning forward—not falling backwards.

814 Never eat liver at a restaurant. Some things should be done only in the privacy of one's home.

815 Clean out a different drawer in your house every week.

816 Share your knowledge. It's a way to achieve immortality.

817 # Be gentle
with the Earth.

꧁

818 Keep impeccable tax records.

819 Don't work for a company led by someone of questionable character.

820 When working with contractors, include a penalty clause in your contract for their not finishing on time.

821 Read bulletin boards at the grocery store, college bookstore, and coin laundry. You will find all sorts of interesting things there.

822 Learn three knock-knock jokes so that you will always be ready to entertain children.

823 The next time you're standing next to a police officer, firefighter, or paramedic, tell them that you appreciate what they do for the community.

824 Visit your old high school and introduce yourself to the principal. Ask if you can sit in on a couple of classes.

825 Show respect when riding sailboats, snowmobiles, and motorcycles. They can teach you a painful lesson very fast.

826 Act with courtesy and fairness regardless of how others treat you. Don't let them determine your response.

827   Spend your time and energy creating, not criticizing.

828   In a verbal confrontation, lower your voice to the degree that the other person raises his or hers.

829   Let your children see you do things for your wife that lets them know how much you love and treasure her.

830   Take photographs of every car you own. Later, these photos will trigger wonderful memories.

831   Don't allow children to ride in the back of a pickup truck.

832 When you are a dinner guest at a restaurant, don't order anything more expensive than your host does.

833 When someone offers to pay you now or later, choose now.

834 Don't leave hair in the shower drain.

835 Start every day with the most important thing you have to do. Save the less important tasks for later.

836 When traveling the backroads, stop whenever you see a sign that reads "Honey For Sale."

837 Think twice before deciding not to charge for your work. People often don't value what they don't pay for.

838 Don't outlive your money.

839 Never grab at a falling knife.

840 When there is a hill to climb, don't think that waiting will make it smaller.

841 When your dog dies, frame his collar and put it above a window facing west.

842 When a garment label warns "Dry Clean Only," believe it.

843   Never take what you cannot use.

844   Don't eat any meat loaf but your mom's.

845   Write the date and the names of non-family members on the backs of all photos as soon as you get them from the developer.

846   Just because you earn a decent wage, don't look down on those who don't. To put things in perspective, consider what would happen to the public good if you didn't do your job for 30 days. Then, consider the consequences if sanitation workers didn't do their jobs for 30 days. Now, whose job is more important?

847 Pray. There is immeasurable power in it.

848 Help a child plant a small garden.

849 Don't take 11 items to the 10 Items Express
Check-Out lane.

850 Don't call a fishing rod a "pole," a line a "rope,"
a rifle a "gun," or a ship a "boat."

851 At meetings, resist turning around to see who
has just arrived late.

852 Don't ride a bicycle or motorcycle barefooted.

853 Refuse to share personal and financial
information unless you feel it is absolutely
essential.

854 Don't purchase anything in a package that appears to have been opened.

855 Never do business with people who knock on your door and say, "I just happened to be in the neighborhood."

856 Don't buy a house in a neighborhood where you have to pay first before pumping gas.

857 Overestimate travel time by 15 percent.

858 Make duplicates of all important keys.

859 Read a lot when you're on vacation, but nothing that has to do with your business.

860 Call a nursing home or retirement center and ask for a list of the residents who seldom get mail or visitors. Send them a card several times a year. Sign it, "Someone who thinks you are very special."

861 Put the knife in the jelly before putting it in the peanut butter when you make a sandwich.

862 Choose a business partner the way you choose a tennis partner. Select someone who's strong where you are weak.

863 Get a haircut at least a week before the big interview.

864 Remember that what's right isn't always popular, and what's popular isn't always right.

865 Before buying a house or renting an apartment, check the water pressure by turning on the faucets and the shower and then flushing the toilet.

866 Properly fitting shoes should feel good as soon as you try them on. Don't believe the salesperson who says, "They'll be fine as soon as you break them in."

867 Schedule your bachelor party at least two days before your wedding.

868 Remember that great love and great achievements involve great risk.

869 Spend your life lifting people up, not putting people down.

870 Never interrupt when you're being flattered.

871 Don't pick up after your children. That's their job.

872 Own a cowboy hat.

873 Own a comfortable chair for reading.

874 Own a set of good kitchen knives.

875 In business or in life, don't follow the wagon tracks too closely.

876 Get your name off mailing lists by writing to: Mail Preference Service, P.O. Box 9008, Farmingdale, NY 11735-9008.

877 Never risk what you can't afford to lose.

878 Never buy anything electrical at a flea market.

879 Don't trust a woman who doesn't close her eyes when you kiss her.

880 Never tell a man he's losing his hair. He already knows.

881 Learn to use a needle and thread, a steam iron, and an espresso machine.

882 Remember that the "suggested retail price" seldom is.

883 Never say, "My child would never do that."

884 Once a year, go someplace you've never been before.

885 Replace the batteries in smoke alarms every January 1st.

886 Never order chicken-fried steak in a place that doesn't have a jukebox.

887 Keep candles and matches in the kitchen and bedroom in case of power failure.

888   Remember that ignorance is expensive.

889   Brush your teeth before putting on your tie.

890   If you make a lot of money, put it to use helping others while you are living. That is wealth's greatest satisfaction.

891   Listen to your critics. They will keep you focused and innovative.

892   Never tell a person who's experiencing deep sorrow, "I know how you feel." You don't.

893   Remember that not getting what you want is sometimes a stroke of good luck.

894 Never say anything to a news reporter that you don't want to see on the front page of your local paper. Comments made "off the record" seldom are.

895 Remember the old proverb, "Out of debt, out of danger."

896 Don't allow your dog to bark and disturb the neighbors.

897 When declaring your rights, don't forget your responsibilities.

898 Dress respectfully when attending church.

899 Remember that what you give will afford you more pleasure than what you get.

900 Display your street number prominently on your mailbox or house in case emergency vehicles need to find you.

901 Think twice before accepting a job that requires you to work in an office with no windows.

902 Never hire someone you wouldn't invite home to dinner.

903 Perform your job better than anyone else can. That's the best job security I know.

904 When camping or hiking, never leave evidence that you were there.

905 Never ask an accountant, lawyer, or doctor professional questions in a social setting.

906 When someone has provided you with exceptional service, write a note to his or her boss.

907 When you've learned that a good friend is ill, don't ask him about it. Let him tell you first.

908 For easier reading in motel rooms, pack your own 100-watt light bulb.

909   Remember that everyone you meet wears an invisible sign. It reads, "Notice me. Make me feel important."

910   When lending people money, be sure their character exceeds their collateral.

911   Whether it's life or a horse that throws you, get right back on.

912   Be cautious telling people how contented and happy you are. Many will resent it.

913   Hang up if someone puts you on hold to take a "call waiting."

914 Learn the rules.
Then break some.

915 Accept the fact that regardless of how many times you are right, you will sometimes be wrong.

916 Every once in a while ask yourself the question, If money weren't a consideration, what would I like to be doing?

917 No matter how old you get, hug and kiss your mother whenever you greet her.

918 Watch *The Andy Griffith Show* to help keep things in perspective.

919 Put love notes in your child's lunch box.

920 Go to rodeos.

921 Go to donkey basketball games.

922 Go to chili cook-offs.

923 Order an L. L. Bean catalog. Write to L. L. Bean, Freeport, ME 04033.

924 Remember that the best relationship is one where your love for each other is greater than your need for each other.

925 When you need assistance, ask this way: "I've got a problem. I wonder if you would be kind enough to help me?"

926 Encourage anyone who is trying to improve mentally, physically, or spiritually.

927 Remember that half the joy of achievement is in the anticipation.

928 Get involved with your local government. As someone said, "Politics is too important to be left to the politicians."

929 Never swap your integrity for money, power, or fame.

930 Call your local police department and ask about riding with an officer on night patrol.

931 Order a Sundance catalog. Write to Customer Service Center, 1909 South 4250 West, Salt Lake City, UT 84104.

932 Never sell yourself short.

933 Fool someone on April 1st.

934 Never remind someone of a kindness or act of generosity you have shown him or her. Bestow a favor and then forget it.

935 Help your children set up their own savings and checking accounts by age 16.

936 Learn to play "Amazing Grace" on the piano.

937 Put on old clothes before you get out the paint brushes.

938 Never be ashamed of your patriotism.

939 Never be ashamed of honest tears.

940 Never be ashamed of laughter that's too loud or singing that's too joyful.

941 Always try the house dressing.

942 Don't trust your memory; write it down.

943 When you get really angry, stick your hands in your pockets.

944 Do all you can to increase the salaries of good teachers.

945 At least once, date a woman with beautiful red hair.

946 Visit friends and relatives when they are in the hospital. You only need to stay a few minutes.

947 Answer the easy questions first.

948 Never leave a youngster in the car without taking the car keys.

949 Don't think that sending a gift or flowers substitutes for your presence.

950 Judge your success by what you had to give up in order to get it.

951 When visiting a small town at lunch time, choose the café on the square.

952 Attach a small Christmas wreath to your car's grill on the first day of December.

953 Never ask a barber if you need a haircut.

954 Truth is serious business. When criticizing others, remember that a little goes a long way.

955 Never buy a piece of jewelry that costs more than $100 without doing a little haggling.

956 When your children are learning to play musical instruments, buy them good ones.

957 Watch the movie *Regarding Henry.*

958 Watch the movie *Mr. Smith Goes to Washington.*

959 Never "borrow" so much as a pencil from your workplace.

960 Become a tourist for a day in your own hometown. Take a tour. See the sights.

961 Don't confuse foolishness with bravery.

962 Don't mistake kindness for weakness.

963 Don't discuss domestic problems at work.

964 Create a smoke-free office and home.

965 Never ignore evil.

966 A racehorse that consistently runs just a second faster than another horse is worth millions of dollars more. Be willing to give that extra effort that separates the winner from the one in second place.

967 Be especially courteous and patient with older people.

968 Remember this statement by Coach Lou Holtz: "Life is 10 percent what happens to me and 90 percent how I react to it."

969 Travel. See new places, but remember to take along an open mind.

970 Let some things remain mysterious.

971 Never get a tattoo.

972 Never eat a sugared doughnut when wearing a dark suit.

973 Call before dropping in on friends and family.

974 When you are away from home and hear church bells, think of someone who loves you.

975 When friends offer to help, let them.

976 Never decide to do nothing just because you can only do a little. Do what you can.

977 Approach love and cooking with reckless abandon.

978 Every now and then, bite off more than you can chew.

979 Remember that your character is your destiny.

980 Grind it out. Hanging on just one second longer than your competition makes you the winner.

981 Be better prepared than you think you need to be.

982 Buy a small, inexpensive camera. Take it with you everywhere.

983 Let your handshake be as binding as a signed contract.

984 Acknowledge every gift, no matter how small.

985 Buy and use your customers' products.

986 Keep and file the best business letters you receive.

987 Get a flu shot.

988 Worry makes for a hard pillow. When something's troubling you, before going to sleep, jot down three things you can do the next day to help solve the problem.

989 Pay the extra money for the best seats at a play or concert.

990 Give handout materials after your presentation, never before.

991 Never buy anything from a rude salesperson, no matter how much you want it.

992 Buy a red umbrella. It's easier to find among all the black ones, and it adds a little color to rainy days.

993 Hire people more for their judgment than for their talents.

994 Every so often, go where you can hear a wooden screen door slam shut.

995 Love someone who doesn't deserve it.

996 When you mean no, say it in a way that's not ambiguous.

997 Attend a high school football game. Sit near the band.

998 Give children toys that are powered by their imagination, not by batteries.

999 Remember that your child's character is like good soup. Both are homemade.

1000 When you're buying something that you only need to buy once, buy the best you can afford.

1001 Never open a restaurant.

1002 As soon as you get married, start saving for your children's education.

1003 Get involved with Habitat for Humanity and help build housing for the poor. Call 1-800-HABITAT.

1004 You may dress unconventionally, but remember, the more strangely you dress, the better you have to be.

1005 Life is short.
Eat more pancakes
and fewer rice cakes.

1006 Reject and condemn prejudice based on race, gender, religion, or age.

1007 Choose a seat in the row next to the emergency exit when flying. You will get more leg room.

1008 Be suspicious of a boss who schedules meetings instead of making decisions.

1009 Carry three business cards in your wallet.

1010 Regardless of the situation, react with class.

1011 For emergencies, always have a quarter in your pocket and a ten-dollar bill hidden in your wallet.

1012 Be able to hit consistently four out of five at the free-throw line.

1013 Don't overfeed horses or brothers-in-law.

1014 Become the kind of person who brightens a room just by entering it.

1015 Remember the observation of William James that the deepest principle in human nature is the craving to be appreciated.

1016 Buy raffle tickets, candy bars, and baked goods from students who are raising money for school projects.

1017   Be wary of the man who's "all hat and no cattle."

1018   Borrow a box of puppies for an afternoon and take them to visit the residents of a retirement home. Stand back and watch the smiles.

1019   Reread Thoreau's *Walden*.

1020   When there's a piano to be moved, don't reach for the stool.

1021   Someone will always be looking at you as an example of how to behave. Don't let that person down.

1022 Go on blind dates. Remember, that's how I met your mother.

1023 Root for the home team.

1024 Follow your own star.

1025 Remember the ones who love you.

1026 Go home for the holidays.

1027 Don't get too big for your britches.

1028 Call your dad.

VOLUME THREE

1029 Never buy a coffee table you can't put your feet on.

1030 Say something positive as early as possible every day.

1031 Believe in miracles but don't depend on them.

1032 Regardless of the situation, remember that nothing is ever lost by courtesy.

1033 Fill out expense reports the day you return from your trip.

1034 Own at least one article of clothing with Mickey Mouse on it.

1035 Never open the refrigerator when you're bored.

1036 Be thankful you were born in this great country.

1037 When staying at a hotel or motel, don't accept a room next to the ice or vending machines.

1038 Enjoy the satisfaction that comes from doing little things well.

1039 If you are involved in an automobile accident, don't admit fault (there may be extenuating circumstances) and don't discuss the accident with anyone except the police and your insurance agent.

1040 Never go near a kid who's holding a water hose unless you want to get wet.

1041 Never refuse a holiday dessert.

1042 Encourage your children to join a choir.

1043 Never allow anyone to intimidate you.

1044 Watch your finances like a hawk.

1045 Don't forget that we are ultimately judged by what we give, not by what we get.

1046 Never complain about the music in someone else's car when you're a passenger.

1047 Always compliment
flower gardens and
new babies.

1048   Read Tom Peter's *The Pursuit of WOW!* (Vantage, 1994).

1049   Remember that it's better to be cheated in price than in quality.

1050   When reading self-help books, include the Bible.

1051   Each year, take a first-day-of-school photograph of your children.

1052   When you hear a kind word spoken about a friend, tell him so.

1053   Pack a couple of Ziploc bags and a pad of Post-it notes when you travel.

1054 Learn the rules of any sport your children play.

1055 Never hesitate to do what you know is right.

1056 Don't work for recognition, but do work worthy of recognition.

1057 Share your knowledge and experiences.

1058 Be charitable in your speech, actions, and judgment.

1059 Work for a company where the expectations of you are high.

1060 Remember that a kind word goes a long way.

1061   Don't allow your children or grandchildren to call you by your first name.

1062   Don't compare your children with their siblings or classmates.

1063   Be enthusiastic in your expressions of gratitude and appreciation.

1064   Join the Rotary or another civic club.

1065   When no great harm will result, let your children do it their way, even if you know they are wrong. They will learn more from their mistakes than from their successes.

1066   Ask permission before taking someone's photograph.

1067   Tell your wife often how terrific she looks.

1068   Never give an anniversary gift that has to be plugged in.

1069   Take some silly photos of yourself and a friend in an instant photo booth.

1070   Remember that regardless of where you are, not much good happens after midnight.

1071   Remember that the word *discipline* means "to teach."

1072   Forgive quickly.

1073   Kiss slowly.

1074   Volunteer to be a Little League umpire.

1075   Remember that all success comes at a price.

1076   When you give someone a camera as a gift, make sure it's loaded with film and has a battery.

1077   Tour your state capitol building.

1078   Own your own tuxedo.

1079   Never say anything uncomplimentary about your wife in the presence of your children.

1080   Earn your success based on service to others, not at the expense of others.

1081 To fight the blues, try exercising.

1082 Kiss your children good night, even if they are already asleep.

1083 Remember the three universal healers: calamine lotion, warm oatmeal, and hugs.

1084 Compliment the parent when you observe a well-behaved child.

1085 When traveling, sleep with your wallet, car keys, room key, eyeglasses, and shoes nearby.

1086 Spend twice as much time praising as you do criticizing.

1087 Never watch a movie or video with your children that involves activities and language that you don't want them to imitate.

1088 Never pass up a chance to be in a parade.

1089 Start the standing ovation at the end of school plays.

1090 Remember the credo of Walt Disney: Think. Believe. Dream. Dare.

1091 When someone lets you down, don't give up on them.

1092 Learn the Heimlich maneuver.

1093 Treat your company's money as you would your own.

1094 Remember that life's big changes rarely give advance warning.

1095 Teach your children never to underestimate someone with a disability.

1096 What you have to do, do wholeheartedly.

1097 Never comment on someone's weight unless you know it's what they want to hear.

1098 Find a job you love and give it everything you've got.

1099 Read the *Wall Street Journal* regularly.

1100 Keep good financial records.

1101 Never complain about a flight delayed for mechanical repairs. Waiting on the ground is infinitely better than the alternative.

1102 Make a list of travel necessities, laminate it, and keep it in your suitcase.

1103 Set limits on the amount and content of television your children watch.

1104 Never forget that it takes only one person or one idea to change your life forever.

1105   Seek respect rather than popularity.

1106   Seek quality rather than luxury.

1107   Seek refinement rather than fashion.

1108   Don't hand out your troubles to your friends and co-workers.

1109   Occasionally let your children help you, even if it slows you down.

1110   Throw a surprise birthday party for a friend.

1111   Report unethical business practices to your city's Better Business Bureau.

1112 Call (800) 525-9000 for a catalog of Nightingale Conant tapes on personal development and achievement.

1113 Start a "smile file" of jokes, articles, and cartoons that make you laugh.

1114 Start a "read again file" for articles you might want to enjoy a second time.

1115 When you need a little advice, call your grandparents.

1116 Teach your sons as well as your daughters to cook.

1117 Remember that when your mom says, "You'll regret it," you probably will.

1118 Always take your vacation time.

1119 Look for the opportunity that's hidden in every adversity.

1120 Don't be critical of your wife's friends.

1121 Be prompt when picking up or dropping off your children for school or other activities.

1122 Take your teenagers with you when you buy a car or expensive household item and let them learn from the experience.

1123 Make a big batch of Rice Krispies squares. Take them to the office.

1124 Don't sit while ladies are standing.

1125 Become a serious student of American history.

1126 Play catch with a kid.

1127 Write some poetry.

1128 Shoot a few hoops.

1129 Once a month invite someone to lunch who knows more about your business than you.

1130 Never ignore an old barking dog.

1131 To open a bottle of champagne, twist the neck, not the cork.

1132 To put someone in your debt, do something nice for their child.

1133 Improve even the best sausage biscuit by spreading on a little grape jelly.

1134 Try to add a new name to your Rolodex every week.

1135 If you are not going to use a discount coupon, leave it on the shelf with the product for someone else to use.

1136 Never criticize your country when traveling abroad.

1137   Respect your elders.

1138   When loved ones drive away, watch until you can no longer see the car.

1139   On your birthday, send your mom a thank-you card.

1140   Never tell an off-color joke in the presence of women or children.

1141   Keep a pad and pencil by every phone.

1142   Spend a couple of hours each week reading magazines that have nothing to do with your job or lifestyle.

1143 Never let the odds keep you from pursuing what you know in your heart you were meant to do.

1144　If you dial a wrong number, don't just hang up; offer an apology.

1145　Hold yourself to the same high standards that you require of others.

1146　If you are a guest at a wedding, take lots of snapshots and send them along with the negatives to the bride and groom as quickly as you can. They have a long time to wait for the formal pictures and will be thrilled to receive the ones you took.

1147　Never loan your chain saw, your ball glove, or your favorite book.

1148 Wage war against procrastination.

1149 Don't open anyone else's mail.

1150 Type out your favorite quotation and place it where you can see it every day.

1151 When playing a sport with a partner, never criticize his or her performance.

1152 Until your children move out of your house, don't buy anything suede.

1153 When the best in the world visits your town for a concert, exhibition, or speech, get tickets to attend.

1154   Learn the techniques of being a good interviewer.

1155   Listen to rumors, but don't contribute any of your own.

1156   Enter something in the state fair.

1157   Offer hope.

1158   Let your word be your bond.

1159   Count your change.

1160   Remember that a lasting marriage is built on commitment, not convenience.

1161 When you need to apologize to someone, do it in person.

1162 Try to find a copy of the book *Under My Elm* by David Grayson (Doubleday, 1942). You might have to order it.

1163 Take your child on a tour of a local university.

1164 Finish projects before they are due.

1165 Never ask a childless couple when they are going to have children.

1166 Let your children observe your being generous to those in need.

1167 Be happy with what you have while working for what you want.

1168 Celebrate even small victories.

1169 Never answer a reporter's questions with, "No comment." Instead, say, "I don't have enough information to comment on that right now."

1170 Cut your toenails in private.

1171 After going to bed, refuse to worry about problems until the morning.

1172 Attend an Eagle Scout's or a Girl Scout's Golden Award induction ceremony.

1173 Never tell a car salesman how much you want to spend.

1174   Return shopping carts to the designated areas.

1175   Redeem gift certificates promptly.

1176   Remember that a grateful heart is almost always a happy one.

1177   Make every effort to attend weddings and funerals.

1178   Don't forget that a couple of words of praise or encouragement can make someone's day.

1179   Every year, send your old alma mater a few bucks.

1180   Make your money before spending it.

1181   Be especially courteous to receptionists and secretaries; they are the gate-keepers.

1182   Don't overschedule your children's extracurricular activities.

1183   Whenever you hear an ambulance siren, say a prayer for the person inside.

1184   Worry about the consequences of the choices you make before you make them—not afterward.

1185   Attend parent-teacher conferences and PTA meetings.

1186   Don't take medicine in the dark.

1187 Spoil your wife,
not your children.

1188 Stop and look up when anyone approaches your desk.

1189 Search out good values, but let the other guy make a fair profit on what you purchase.

1190 Get a passport and keep it current.

1191 Be cautious of renting lodging accommodations described in the ad or brochure as "rustic."

1192 Insist that your children complete a driver's education course at their school.

1193 Locate the emergency exits on your floor as soon as you check into your hotel room.

1194 Never pass up a chance to jump on a trampoline.

1195 Get to know your children's teachers.

1196 Stay humble.

1197 Stay on your toes.

1198 Hang up on anyone you don't know who's trying to sell you a financial product over the telephone.

1199 Buy each of your children a special Christmas ornament every year. When they move into their own homes, box up the ornaments and give them as house-warming gifts.

1200 Remember that you can miss a lot of good things in life by having the wrong attitude.

1201   Support your local museums.

1202   Support your local symphony.

1203   Support your community college.

1204   When a guest, never complain about the food, drink, or accommodations.

1205   Take a course in public speaking.

1206   Write a letter to the editor at least once a year.

1207   For better security when traveling, take along a small wedge of wood and jam it under your hotel room door.

1208 Know where to find a gas station that's open twenty-four hours with a working bathroom.

1209 Never criticize a gift.

1210 Never leave a loved one in anger.

1211 Keep a roll of duct tape at home, at the office, and in your car.

1212 Require your children to do their share of household chores.

1213 When in doubt, smile.

1214 Toss in a coin when passing a wishing well.

1215 Underestimate when guessing an adult's age or weight.

1216 Overestimate when guessing someone's salary.

1217 Choose a clothing salesperson who dresses as you wish you did.

1218 Send notes of encouragement to military personnel and college students.

1219 Occasionally leave a quarter in the change return slot of a pay phone. Somebody always checks.

1220 Overpay the neighborhood kid who does yard work for you.

1221　When a friend is in need, help him without his having to ask.

1222　Keep an empty gas can in your trunk.

1223　Own a salad spinner.

1224　Own two crystal champagne glasses.

1225　Allow drivers from out of state a little extra room on the road.

1226　When serving hamburgers, always toast the buns.

1227　Never whittle toward yourself.

1228 Make a generous contribution to diabetes research.

1229 Teach your children the pride, satisfaction, and dignity of doing any job well.

1230 Never ask a woman when the baby is due unless you know for sure that she's pregnant.

1231 Frame anything your child brings home on his first day of school.

1232 Host a backyard get-together for friends and neighbors every Labor Day.

1233 Keep $10 in your glove box for emergencies.

1234 Never be too busy
to meet someone new.

1235 Volunteer to help at your city's Special Olympics.

1236 Surprise someone who's more than eighty years old or a couple celebrating fifty years or more of marriage with a personal greeting from the President. Mail details to The White House, Greetings Office, Room 39, Washington, DC 20500, four to six weeks in advance.

1237 If it's not a beautiful morning, let your cheerfulness make it one.

1238 Don't say anything on a cordless or cellular telephone that you don't want the world to hear.

1239　Remember that cruel words deeply hurt.

1240　Remember that loving words quickly heal.

1241　Plant a tree the day your child is born.

1242　Never get yourself into a position where you have to back up a trailer.

1243　Marry someone your equal or a little bit better.

1244　Keep a special notebook. Every night before going to bed, make a note of something beautiful that you saw during the day.

1245　When you're the first one up, be quiet about it.

1246   This year, visit two or three of your state parks.

1247   Remember that a minute of anger denies you sixty seconds of happiness.

1248   Include a recent family photo when writing to a loved one.

1249   Ask your grandparents to tell you stories about your parents while they were growing up.

1250   Welcome the unexpected! Opportunities rarely come in neat, predictable packages.

1251   Before criticizing a new employee, remember your first days at work.

1252 To help your children turn out well, spend twice as much time with them and half as much money.

1253 Become a Big Brother or Big Sister.

1254 Give young children the opportunity to participate in family decision-making. Their insight will surprise you.

1255 Tell family members you love them before they go away for a few days.

1256 Keep a backup copy of your personal address book.

1257 Fill out customer comment cards.

1258 Mail in your Publishers Clearing House sweepstakes notice. Who knows?

1259 Don't make eating everything on their plate an issue with children.

1260 Never miss an opportunity to go fishing with your father.

1261 Never miss an opportunity to go traveling with your mother.

1262 Hold a child's hand when crossing the street.

1263 Do something every day that maintains your good health.

1264 When traveling, stop occasionally at local cafés and diners.

1265 Never deny anyone the opportunity to do something nice for you.

1266 Never tell a woman you liked her hair better before she had it cut.

1267 When playing golf and tennis, occasionally play with someone better than you are.

1268 Dust, then vacuum.

1269 Offer to pay for parking and tolls when you ride with someone.

1270 Offer to leave the tip when someone invites you out to eat.

1271　Every spring set out a couple of tomato plants.

1272　Visit a pet store every once in a while and watch the children watch the animals.

1273　Remember that a successful future begins right now.

1274　Don't minimize your child's worries and fears.

1275　Take advantage of free lectures on any subject in which you are remotely interested.

1276　Never give up on a dream just because of the length of time it will take to accomplish it. The time will pass anyway.

1277 Hold puppies, kittens, and babies any time you get the chance.

1278 Memorize the names of the books of the Bible.

1279 Memorize the names and order of the Presidents.

1280 Take Trivial Pursuit cards to read to the driver on a long road trip. It makes the time fly.

1281 After children argue and have apologized, ask each one to say something nice about the other.

1282 Watch your back.

1283 Watch your weight.

1284 Watch your language.

1285   Never forget the debt you owe to all those who have come before you.

1286   Remember that anything creative and innovative will be copied.

1287   When traveling, pack more underwear and socks than you think you will need.

1288   Dress for the position you want, not the one you have.

1289   Keep a couple of your favorite inspirational books by your bedside.

1290   Never ignore a ringing fire alarm.

1291   Don't write down anything you don't want
       someone else to read.

1292   Whisper in your sleeping child's ear, "I love
       you."

1293   At least once in your life, see the Grand Teton
       Mountains from the back of a horse.

1294   When taking a true-false test, remember that
       any statement that includes the word *any*, *all*,
       always, *never*, or *ever* is usually false.

1295   Let your children know that regardless of what
       happens, you'll always be there for them.

1296 Use good stationery when you want your written comments to be taken seriously.

1297 Unless it creates a safety problem, pull your car over and stop when a funeral procession is passing.

1298 Keep a blanket in the trunk of your car for emergencies during the winter months.

1299 Take a ride in a glider.

1300 Take a ride in a hot-air balloon.

1301 Be the first to apologize to a family member after a disagreement.

1302   Ask your boss what he expects of you.

1303   To find out who is behind an idea or activity, follow the money.

1304   If you borrow something more than twice, buy one for yourself.

1305   When you build a home, make sure it has a screened-in porch.

1306   Be innovative.

1307   Be passionate.

1308   Be committed.

1309   Be the first adult to jump into the pool or run into the ocean with the kids. They will love you for it.

1310   Don't play your car stereo so loud that you can't hear approaching emergency vehicles.

1311   Become knowledgeable about antiques, oriental rugs, and contemporary art.

1312   Don't get caught glancing at your watch when you're talking to someone.

1313   Every December, give the world a precious gift. Give a pint of blood.

1314 Remember that life's most treasured moments often come unannounced.

1315   Never tell anybody they don't have a good sense of humor.

1316   Never tell anybody they can't sing.

1317   When parents introduce you to their children, say, "I have looked forward to meeting you, because your parents are always bragging about you."

1318   Before buying that all-important engagement ring, find out all you can about diamonds by calling (800) 340-3028. The American Gem Society will send you a booklet that will answer some of your questions.

1319 Call a radio talk show with an opinion.

1320 Don't argue with your mother.

1321 Clear the adding machine after using it.

1322 Plant a couple of fruit trees in your back yard.

1323 Wear a tie with cartoon characters on it if you work with kids.

1324 Remember that every age brings new opportunities.

1325 Eat lightly or not at all before giving a speech or making a presentation.

1326 Attend family reunions and be patient when aunts and uncles want to take your picture.

1327 Go for long, hand-holding walks with your wife.

1328 Visit the Biltmore estate in Asheville, North Carolina, during the spring tulip festival.

1329 Ask an older person you respect to tell you his or her proudest moment and greatest regret.

1330 Record the birthday heights of your children on the kitchen doorjamb. Never paint it.

1331 Every once in a while, let your kids play in the rain.

1332 Become the world's most thoughtful friend.

1333   When a woman is in the hospital, give her a soft, stuffed animal instead of flowers.

1334   Always order bread pudding when it's on the menu.

1335   Create and maintain a peaceful home.

1336   Never ask anyone why they wear a Medic Alert bracelet. That's his or her business.

1337   Tell gardeners of public areas how much you appreciate the beauty they bring to your city.

1338   When taking family photos, include a few routine, everyday shots.

1339   Remember that anything worth doing is going to take longer than you think.

1340   Know your children's friends.

1341   No matter how angry you get with your wife, never sleep apart.

1342   Carry a kite in the trunk for windy spring days.

1343   Buy a flashlight for each person in your family to keep in their bedroom.

1344   Own a world globe.

1345   Own a good set of encyclopedia.

1346 Teach a Sunday school class.

1347 Never call anybody stupid, even if you're kidding.

1348 Find something that's important to your company and learn to do it better than anyone else.

1349 Don't eat anything covered with chocolate unless you know what's inside.

1350 Don't eat anything covered with gravy unless you know what's under it.

1351 Don't drink anything blue.

1352 Never marry someone in hope that they'll change later.

1353 Buy your mom flowers and your dad a new tie with your first paycheck.

1354 Be prudent.

1355 Be positive.

1356 Be polite.

1357 Criticize the behavior, not the person.

1358 Never leave fun to find fun.

1359 Keep receipts.

1360 Rebuild a broken relationship.

1361 Keep a photograph of each person you have dated.

1362 Keep a current city and state highway map in your car's glove box.

1363 Ever wonder what it takes to become an astronaut? Receive the application package by writing to NASA, Johnson Space Center, Attn: AHX Astronaut Selection Office, Houston, TX 77059.

1364 If you live in the same city as your mother-in-law, occasionally trim her hedges and wash her car.

1365   Don't buy cheap picture frames.

1366   Don't buy a cheap tennis racket.

1367   Don't buy a cheap motorcycle helmet.

1368   When traveling, always pack a white dress shirt and a tie.

1369   Collect seashells from your favorite beach.

1370   Collect menus from your favorite restaurants.

1371   Notify the manager when a restaurant's restroom isn't clean.

1372   Learn to make corn bread in a cast-iron skillet.

1373 When traveling, carry the phone number and address of your destination in your wallet.

1374 On long-distance road trips, make sure that someone besides the driver stays awake.

1375 Treat yourself to a professional shoeshine the next time you're at the airport.

1376 At least once a month, get real dirty and sweaty.

1377 Ask your child to read a bedtime story to you for a change.

1378 Play Monopoly with your in-laws. It will reveal a lot about them.

1379 Give a trusted auto technician all your repairs, not just the tough ones.

1380 Write a letter of encouragement to the President—even if he didn't get your vote.

1381 Find a creative florist and give them all your business.

1382 Buy an inexpensive Polaroid camera. Sometimes you don't want to wait even an hour to see the pictures.

1383 Send Valentines to your children as well as to your wife.

1384 When eating cinnamon rolls or prime rib, eat the center portion first.

1385 Add postscripts to your letters. Make them sweet and kind.

1386 Remember that bad luck as well as good luck seldom lasts long.

1387 Never let anyone challenge you to drive faster than you think is safe.

1388 Offer your place in line at the grocery checkout if the person behind you has only two or three items.

1389   Stop at the visitor's information center when entering a state for the first time.

1390   When you see someone sitting alone on a bench, make it a point to speak to them.

1391   Wet your hands before lifting a trout from the river.

1392   Don't force machinery.

1393   When walking a dog, let the dog pick the direction.

1394   Teach your children that when they divide something, the other person gets first pick of the two pieces.

1395 Never give a friend's or relative's name or phone number to a telephone solicitor.

1396 When going to buy a car, leave your good watch at home.

1397 Don't be so open-minded that your brains fall out.

1398 Stand up when an elderly person enters the room.

1399 Put a love note in your wife's luggage before she leaves on a trip.

1400 This year, buy an extra box of Girl Scout cookies.

1401 Exercise caution the first day you buy a chain saw. You'll be tempted to cut down everything in the neighborhood.

1402   Never buy an article of clothing thinking it will fit if you lose a couple of pounds.

1403   Root for your team to win, not for the other team to lose.

1404   Be grateful that God doesn't answer all your prayers.

1405   Accept triumph and defeat with equal grace.

1406   Always watch the high school bands' halftime performances. They practiced just as hard as the football players.

1407   Never set a drink down on a book.

1408   Listen to your favorite music while working on your tax return.

1409   Eat at a truck stop.

1410   Sniff an open bottle of suntan lotion and a fresh lime to temporarily curb the winter blues.

1411   Never give a pet as a surprise gift.

1412   When a child is selling something for a dime, give a quarter.

1413   When you move into a new house, plant a rosebush and put out a new welcome mat to make it seem like home.

1414 After someone apologizes to you, don't lecture them.

1415 Never ignore your car's oil warning light.

1416 Make your wedding anniversary an all-day celebration.

1417 Blow a kiss when driving away from loved ones.

1418 Carry a couple of inexpensive umbrellas in your car that you can give to people caught in the rain.

1419 Be willing to swap a temporary inconvenience for a permanent improvement.

1420 Never order barbecue
in a restaurant where
all the chairs match.

1421 When you complete a course, shake the instructor's hand and thank him or her.

1422 Contribute something to each Salvation Army kettle you pass during the holidays.

1423 Regarding rental property, remember that an unrented house is better than a bad tenant.

1424 Carry a small Swiss Army knife on your key chain.

1425 When you really like someone, tell them. Sometimes you only get one chance.

1426 Take more pictures of people than of places.

1427 Never make fun of people who speak broken English. It means they know another language.

1428 When going through the checkout line, always ask the cashier how she's doing.

1429 Learn and use the four-digit extension to your ZIP code.

1430 When you need something done, ask a busy person.

1431 Send a "thinking of you" card to a friend who's experiencing the anniversary of the loss of a loved one.

1432 Call three friends on Thanksgiving and tell them how thankful you are for their friendship.

1433 Read acknowledgments, introductions, and prefaces to books.

1434 Never underestimate the influence of the people you have allowed into your life.

1435 Enter a room or meeting like you own the place.

1436 Refinish a piece of furniture. Just once.

1437 When you are angry with someone, write a letter telling him or her why you feel that way—but don't mail it.

1438 Learn your great-grandparents' names and what they did.

1439 Don't use your teeth to open things.

1440 When visiting state and national parks, take advantage of all tours and lectures given by park rangers.

1441 Never keep a free ride waiting.

1442 If you ask someone to do something for you, let them do it their way.

1443 Occasionally walk through old cemeteries and read the gravestones.

1444 Protect your enthusiasm
from the negativity
of others.

1445   When visitors ask, be able to recommend three or four free hometown "must sees."

1446   Call your parents as soon as you return from a long trip.

1447   Catch up on the bestsellers by listening to books on tape in your car.

1448   When someone you know is down and out, mail them a twenty-dollar bill anonymously.

1449   Share the remote control.

1450   When pouring something from one container to another, do it over the sink.

1451   Savor every day.

1452   Once a year take your boss to lunch.

1453   Wave to train engineers.

1454   Learn to paddle a canoe.

1455   Aspirin is aspirin. Buy the least expensive brand.

1456   Don't spend lots of time with couples who criticize each other.

1457   Remember the best way to improve your kids is to improve your marriage.

1458   Never go up a ladder with just one nail.

1459   When moving from a house or apartment, for nostalgia's sake, take a photo of each room while the furniture is still in place.

1460   Stand out from the crowd.

1461   Once in your life, paint a picture.

1462   Never buy a Rolex watch from someone who's out of breath.

1463   Remember, it's not your job to get people to like you, it's your job to like people.

1464   When someone gives you something, never say, "You shouldn't have."

1465   Never fry bacon while naked.

1466   Never squat with your spurs on.

1467   Pay attention to pictures of missing children.

1468   Read biographies of successful men and women.

1469   Offer to say grace at holiday meals.

1470   Never miss a chance to shake hands with Santa.

1471   Remember that the only dumb question is the one you wanted to ask but didn't.

1472   Watch a video on CPR and emergency first aid with your family.

1473 Ask yourself if what you're doing today is getting you closer to where you want to be tomorrow.

1474 When you find a coin on the ground, pick it up and give it to the first person you see.

1475 Add *The Book of Virtues* by William Bennett (Simon & Schuster, 1993) to your home library.

1476 Don't expect different results from the same behavior.

1477 Spend time with lucky people.

1478 Wash whites separately.

1479 Keep a couple of Wet-Naps in the glove box.

1480 Never date anyone who has more than two cats.

1481 Always offer guests something to eat or drink when they drop by.

1482 Treat your parents to a dinner out on your birthday.

1483 Don't look through other people's medicine cabinets, closets, or refrigerators.

1484 Make your bed every morning.

1485 When someone tells you they love you, never say, "No, you don't."

1486 When you race your kids, let them win at the end.

1487   Hug a cow.

1488   Once a summer, run through a yard sprinkler.

1489   For an unforgettable adventure, float the Gauley River in West Virginia.

1490   Remember that nothing important was ever achieved without someone's taking a chance.

1491   Stand up for your high principles even if you have to stand alone.

1492   When babies are born into your family, save the newspaper from that day. Give it to them on their eighteenth birthday.

1493 Never resist
a generous impulse.

1494   Every couple of months, spend thirty minutes or so in a big toy store.

1495   Watch reruns of *The Wonder Years.*

1496   Carefully examine your written work when you are finished.

1497   Even on short ferry rides, always get out of your car and enjoy the crossing.

1498   When on vacation or a family holiday, don't be too concerned about the cost. This is not a time to count pennies; it's a time to make memories.

1499   Be faithful.

1500   Write a thank-you note to your children's teacher when you see your child learning new things.

1501   Support family-run businesses.

1502   Read the *Old Farmer's Almanac.*

1503   Remember that everyone has bad days.

1504   Learn to eat with chopsticks.

1505   Add *Art of the Western World* to your videocassette collection.

1506   Never sharpen a boomerang.

1507   Never intentionally embarrass anyone.

1508 Eat moderately.

1509 Exercise vigorously.

1510 When you're angry, take a thirty-minute walk; when you're really angry, chop some firewood.

1511 Be wary of stopping at restaurants displaying Help Wanted signs.

1512 When returning a book or an item of clothing you have borrowed, leave a note of appreciation.

1513 When you pass a family riding in a big U-Haul truck, give them the "thumbs-up" sign. They need all the encouragement they can get.

1514   Question your prejudices.

1515   Have your piano tuned every six months.

1516   Avoid automated teller machines at night.

1517   Make sure the telephone number on your letterhead and business card is large enough to be read easily.

1518   Remember the main thing is to keep the main thing the main thing.

1519   Have your pastor over for dinner.

1520   Be sure the person you marry loves music.

1521 Take your family to a dude ranch for a vacation.

1522 See any detour as an opportunity to experience new things.

1523 When adults are sick, care for them as though they were children.

1524 Watch what you eat at cocktail parties. Each hors d'oeuvre has about one hundred calories.

1525 When deplaning, thank the captain for a safe and comfortable flight.

1526 Never break off communications with your children, no matter what they do.

1527 Learn the history of your hometown.

1528 Remember that wealth is not having all the money you want, but having all the money you need.

1529 Have a little money in the bank to handle unforeseen problems.

1530 Read *Growing a Business* by Paul Hawken (Simon & Schuster, 1987).

1531 Remember that much truth is spoken in jest.

1532 Don't forget that your attitude is just as important as the facts.

1533 Don't live
with the brakes on.

1534 Visit the Art Institute of Chicago.

1535 Take your dad bowling.

1536 Never complain about the food or entertainment at church suppers or charity functions.

1537 When talking to someone who's a new parent, always ask to see a picture of the baby.

1538 Remember that true happiness comes from virtuous living.

1539 Don't obligate yourself to a home mortgage larger than three times your family's annual income.

1540   Take a course in basic car repair.

1541   When asked, take the time to give out-of-town visitors complete and clear directions.

1542   Pass down family recipes.

1543   Ask for advice when you need it, but remember that no one is an expert on your life.

1544   If you know you're going to lose, do it with style.

1545   Remember that creating a successful marriage is like farming; you have to start over again every morning.

1546 Talk to your plants.

1547 Say something every day that encourages your children.

1548 Rescue your dreams.

1549 Teach by example.

1550 Commit yourself to a mighty purpose.

1551 Live simply.

1552 Think quickly.

1553 Work diligently.

1554 Fight fairly.

1555 Give generously.

1556 Laugh loudly.

1557 Love deeply.

1558 Plant more flowers than you pick.

1559 Remember that all important truths are simple.

1560 Include your parents in your prayers.

Dear Reader,

If you received advice from your parents or grandparents that was especially meaningful and would like for me to share it with other readers, please write and tell me about it.

I look forward to hearing from you.

H. Jackson Brown, Jr.
P.O. Box 150115
Nashville, TN 37215